Editor
Eric Migliaccio

Managing Editor
Ina Massler Levin, M.A.

Editor-in-Chief
Sharon Coan, M.S. Ed.

Cover Artist
Barb Lorseyedi

Art Coordinator
Kevin Barnes

Imaging
Alfred Lau
James Edward Grace

Product Manager
Phil Garcia

Publishers
Rachelle Cracchiolo, M.S. Ed.
Mary Dupuy Smith, M.S. Ed.

Practice Makes Perfect
Punctuate & Capitalize

GRADE 1

Includes practice for Standardized Tests

Author

Michelle Breyer, M.A.

Teacher Created Materials, Inc.
6421 Industry Way
Westminster, CA 92683
www.teachercreated.com

ISBN-0-7439-3344-3

©2002 Teacher Created Materials, Inc.
Made in U.S.A.

Table of Contents

Introduction

The old adage "practice makes perfect" can really hold true for your child and his or her education. The more practice and exposure your child has with concepts being taught in school, the more success he or she is likely to find. For many parents, knowing how to help their children may be frustrating because the resources may not be readily available.

As a parent it is also difficult to know where to focus your efforts so that the extra practice your child receives at home supports what he or she is learning in school.

This book has been written to help parents and teachers reinforce basic skills with children. *Practice Makes Perfect: Punctuate and Capitalize, Grade 1* reviews basic skills of punctuation and capitalization for first graders. The exercises in this book can be done sequentially or can be taken out of order, as needed.

The following standards or objectives will be met or reinforced by completing the practice pages included in this book. These standards and objectives are similar to the ones required by your state and school district. These standards and objectives are appropriate for first graders.

- The student correctly uses and capitalizes the pronoun "I."
- The student identifies and correctly capitalizes the first word in a sentence.
- The student identifies and correctly capitalizes simple proper nouns (e.g., names of people, days of the week, months of the year).
- The student identifies different types of sentences (i.e., declarative (telling), interrogative (question), and exclamatory (with emotion).
- The student uses correct punctuation at the end of sentences (i.e., period, question mark, exclamation point).
- The student uses a comma to separate words in a series.
- The student uses a comma to separate adjectives (describing words) describing the same noun.

How to Make the Most of This Book

Here are some useful ideas for making the most of this book:

- Set aside a specific place in your home to work on this book. Keep it neat and tidy, with the necessary materials on hand.
- Set up a certain time of day to work on these practice pages to establish consistency; or look for times in your day or week that are less hectic and conducive to practicing skills.
- Keep all practice sessions with your child positive and constructive. If your child becomes frustrated or tense, set the book aside and look for another time to practice. Forcing your child to perform will not help. Do not use this book as a punishment.
- Help beginning readers with instructions.
- Review the work your child has done.
- Allow the child to use whatever writing instruments he or she prefers. For example, colored pencils can add variety and pleasure to drill work.
- Pay attention to the areas in which your child has the most difficulty. Provide extra guidance and exercises in those areas.
- Look for ways to make real-life application to the skills being reinforced. Play games with your child, looking for nouns or verbs in sentences.

Punctuation and Capitalization Reference Page

Capital Letters

Capitalize the pronoun "I."

    Yesterday **I** went to the movies.

Capitalize the first word of every sentence.

    It's going to rain today.

Capitalize the names of people.

    Abraham **L**incoln was a great president.

Capitalize the days of the week.

    I am buying lunch on **W**ednesday.

Capitalize the months of the year.

    My birthday is in **D**ecember.

Period

A period ends declarative (telling) sentences.

    I like chocolate ice cream**.**

A period ends imperative (command) sentences.

    Shut the door**.**

Question Mark

A question mark ends interrogative sentences (questions).

    When does school start**?**

Exclamation Point

An exclamation point ends exclamatory (with emotion) sentences.

    We won the game**!**

Commas

Commas separate items in a series.

    I like blue, yellow, and green.

Commas separate adjectives (describing words) describing the same noun.

    I saw a big, scary monster.

Capitalize I

Capitalization Rule: Capitalize the pronoun "I."

Fill in the pronoun "I" on the lines below.

1. Last night _____ watched a video.

2. _____ like to play soccer at recess.

3. In my bank _____ have ten dollars.

4. _____ have a pet fish named Space Ranger.

5. My mom and _____ read a good book.

6. _____ am going to the beach.

7. At the library _____ checked out a book on tape.

8. May _____ go to the movies with Sam?

9. _____ went to a baseball game.

10. Yesterday _____ rode my bike to the store.

Things I Do

Capitalization Rule: Capitalize the pronoun "I."

Rewrite the sentences below. Practice making the pronoun "I" a capital letter.

1. i like to eat pizza for dinner.

2. i have a pet rat named Angel.

3. On Friday, i am going to a birthday party.

4. i learned to ride a horse when i was seven.

5. If i eat my vegetables, then i get dessert.

My Favorite Things

Capitalization Rule: Capitalize the pronoun "I."

Answer the following questions about the things that you like. Begin each sentence with "I like." Be sure to capitalize the word "I" and use a complete sentence. The first one is started for you.

1. What is your favorite color?

   _____

   -

   I like the color _____

2. What sports do you like to play?

   _____

   -

   _____

3. What is your favorite dessert?

   _____

   -

   _____

4. Who is your favorite friend?

   _____

   -

   _____

5. What do you like to do after school?

   _____

   -

   _____

6. What is your favorite animal?

   _____

   -

   _____

A Good Start

Capitalization Rule: Capitalize the first word in every sentence.

Circle the first word in each sentence. Then rewrite the word using a capital letter.

1. today we went to the pool. _____

2. we saw many people there. _____

3. did you see her swim across the pool? _____

4. some children played in the water. _____

5. a man dived into the deep end. _____

6. he made a big splash. _____

7. give me a towel to dry off. _____

8. what a fun day at the pool! _____

At School

Capitalization Rule: Capitalize the first word in every sentence.

Rewrite each sentence. Be sure to use a capital letter at the beginning of each sentence.

1. we write in our spelling books.

2. math was easy today!

3. the date is on the chalkboard.

4. today we sang a song about the flag.

5. did you play ball at recess?

Picture Clues

Capitalization Rule: Capitalize the first word in every sentence.

Write a sentence to go with each picture. Be sure to use a capital letter to begin each sentence and a period at the end.

1.

2.

3.

4.

5.

How You Begin

Capitalization Rule: Capitalize the first word in every sentence.

Write a sentence to go with each word. Be sure to use a capital letter to begin each sentence and a period at the end.

1. bike

2. ball

3. jumped

4. play

5. red

6. tall

Proper People

Capitalization Rule: Capitalize proper nouns, such as the names of people.

Circle the name of the person in each sentence. Then rewrite the name using a capital letter. Be sure to capitalize first, middle, and last names.

1. My best friend is richard.

2. kara likes to play with her pet rat.

3. Did you go to the park with colton?

4. I like to ride bikes with jane hill.

5. Give the birthday gift to ted lee.

6. We flew a kite with ben poe.

7. My art teacher is mary gray.

8. sue ann carr won the prize.

9. Address the card to pat ward.

10. Have you seen jim roberts today?

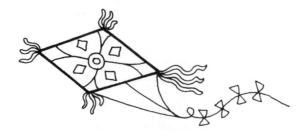

Who Do You Know?

Capitalization Rule: Capitalize proper nouns, such as the names of people.

Practice capitalizing the names of people by writing these sentences on the lines.

1. linda bought some grapes at the store.

2. What did gary do at the beach?

3. Go to the show with matthew morgan.

4. kari knowles is driving down the street.

5. My brother's name is ethan zane emery.

Names of Days

Capitalization Rule: **Capitalize proper nouns, such as the names of the days of the week.**

Write the days of the week in order on the lines below. Be sure to use a capital letter.

saturday   monday   thursday   tuesday   sunday   friday   wednesday

1. _____

2. _____

3. _____

4. _____

5. _____

6. _____

7. _____

Answer the questions about the days of the week. Be sure to begin each day with a capital letter.

1. What day is it today?   _____

2. What day will it be tomorrow?   _____

3. What day was it yesterday?   _____

Weekly Names

Capitalization Rule: **Capitalize proper nouns, such as the names of the days of the week.**

Practice capitalizing the days of the week by writing these sentences on the lines.

1. I have piano lessons on monday.

    _____

    -

    _____

    _____

    -

2. saturday our family went to the beach.

    _____

    -

    _____

    _____

    -

3. Mark is coming over to play on wednesday.

    _____

    -

    _____

    _____

    -

Write a sentence about something you do on Friday. Be sure to include the name of the day in your sentence and use a capital letter.

    _____

    -

    _____

    _____

    -

    _____

    -

    _____

Calendar Names

Capitalization Rule: Capitalize proper nouns, such as the months of the year.

Below is a list of all of the months. Write them in order of the year. Be sure to use a capital letter.

1. _____   7. _____

2. _____   8. _____

3. _____   9. _____

4. _____   10. _____

5. _____   11. _____

6. _____   12. _____

november	september	june	july
april	march	december	august
february	may	october	january

Choose and write a name of a month that belongs with each season. Be sure to use a capital letter.

1. winter _____

2. spring _____

3. summer _____

Monthly Minders

Capitalization Rule: **Capitalize proper nouns, such as the months of the year.**

Practice capitalizing the months of the year by writing these sentences.

1. My birthday is in december.

   _____

   -

   _____

2. We will go to grandma's in may.

   _____

   -

   _____

3. Will you take a trip in july?

   _____

   -

   _____

Write a sentence to go with each picture. Include the name of a month in your sentence.

1.

2.

Capitalize It!

Read each sentence carefully to find words that should be capitalized. Cross out the incorrect letter and write a capital letter above it.

1. this july my family and i are taking a trip to Texas.

2. we will visit our cousins natalie and nile rodgers.

3. i have already begun to plan our july vacation.

4. we will arrive monday at natalie and nile's house.

5. they will take us to the zoo on tuesday and wednesday.

6. then i will visit with my friend teresa linden on thursday.

7. our family will fly home on friday.

8. meredith hemerson will pick us up at the airport friday night.

9. i can't wait until july!

10. do you think we can take one trip in november and one in may?

Capital Caper

Rewrite each sentence properly. Be sure to use capital letters where they are needed.

1. my birthday comes each june.

   _____

   _____

   _____

2. i will go to the park on friday.

   _____

   _____

   _____

3. katie will call sara on Tuesday.

   _____

   _____

   _____

4. on thursday i will call melanie hart.

   _____

   _____

   _____

5. she ran on a wednesday in august.

   _____

   _____

   _____

Can You Capitalize?

Write the correct word in each blank from the choices underneath each sentence. Be sure to use capital letters when they are needed.

1. _____ can you snow ski in _____ ?

july	how	i

2. _____ went to the store on _____ .

tuesday	mike	cat

3. _____ have a dog named _____ .

rex	i	car

4. _____ people work on _____ .

friday	i	some

5. _____ like to play with _____ .

jim	desk	i

6. _____ your birthday in _____ ?

give	is	april

Telling Sentences

Punctuation Rules: **Sentences end with punctuation marks.**

Declarative (telling) sentences end with periods.

Practice writing a period at the end of these declarative sentences.

1. My family has a pet goldfish
2. I watched a movie on Saturday
3. We had noodles for dinner
4. William rides a red scooter

Rewrite each sentence using a period at the end.

1. Our team is the Cobras

2. We won our game

3. I played goalie

4. Our colors are red and black

You Tell It

Punctuation Rules: Sentences end with punctuation marks.

Declarative (telling) sentences end with periods.

Write a declarative (telling) sentence to go with each picture. Be sure to end each sentence with a period.

1. _____

2. _____

3. _____

4. _____

5. _____

Word Clue

Punctuation Rules: Sentences end with punctuation marks.

Declarative (telling) sentences end with periods.

Write your own declarative (telling) sentences using the word clues.
Be sure to end your sentences with periods.

happy   1. _____

pizza   2. _____

blue   3. _____

mad   4. _____

bike   5. _____

Scrambled Sentences

Punctuation Rules: **Sentences end with punctuation marks.**

Declarative (telling) sentences end with periods.

Unscramble these words to make a sentence. Be sure to use a period at the end.

1. house dog A is in his

   _____

2. I ice cream the ate

   _____

3. swim ocean the in Sharks

   _____

4. read I my can book

   _____

5. apple good This a is

   _____

Commands

Punctuation Rules: Sentences end with punctuation marks.

Imperative (command) sentences end with periods.

Practice writing each of these sentences with a period at the end.

1. Turn to page 25 in your book

2. Give me the yellow ball

3. Shut the door gently

Write your own imperative (command) sentences. Be sure to use a period at the end.

1.

2.

Questions

Punctuation Rules: Sentences end with punctuation marks.

Interrogative (questioning) sentences end with question marks.

Place a question mark in the box at the end of each interrogative (questioning) sentence. Then write the first word of each sentence on the blank. What do you notice about each of these sentences?

1. What do you want for dinner ☐ _____

2. Do you know his name ☐ _____

3. Will Kim be at the park ☐ _____

4. Who ate the cookie ☐ _____

5. Why is the sky cloudy ☐ _____

6. Can Marie come out to play ☐ _____

7. When is the movie over ☐ _____

8. How old are you ☐ _____

9. Does Jose know you are here ☐ _____

10. Did you feed the dog ☐ _____

Asking Clues

Punctuation Rules: Sentences end with punctuation marks.

Interrogative (questioning) sentences end with question marks.

Write a question that begins with the word listed on each line. Be sure to end your question with a question mark.

1. Who

2. What

3. When

4. Where

5. Why

6. How

Questions and Answers

Punctuation Rules: Sentences end with punctuation marks.

Declarative (telling) sentences end with periods.

Interrogative (questioning) sentences end with question marks.

Place a period or question mark at the end of each sentence. Then match each question to its answer by drawing a line between the two.

1. Who invented the light bulb

2. Ocean water tastes salty

3. What color is a stop sign

4. Thanksgiving is in November

5. The Statue of Liberty is in New York

A. When is Thanksgiving

B. Thomas Edison invented the light bulb

C. Where is the Statue of Liberty

D. How does ocean water taste

E. A stop sign is red

Write a question. Then write the answer. Be sure to use the proper punctuation at the end of each sentence.

_____
- -
_____
_____
- -
_____
_____
- -
_____
_____
- -
_____

Exclaim It!

Punctuation Rules: Sentences end with punctuation marks.
Declarative (telling) sentences end with periods.
Exclamatory (with emotion) sentences end with exclamation points.

Write a period at the end of the first sentence. Write an exclamation point at the end of the second sentence. Then read each sentence aloud, showing how the emotion of the sentence changes by the tone of your voice.

1. It is the last day of school   It is the last day of school

2. I liked that movie   I liked that movie

3. We won the game   We won the game

4. I passed my math test   I passed my math test

5. My pet snake has escaped   My pet snake has escaped

Practice writing exclamation points in the boxes at the ends of these sentences.

1. Give the basketball to me ☐

2. Look out for the waterfall ☐

3. Be careful with that match ☐

Say It With Feeling

Punctuation Rules: Sentences end with punctuation marks.

Exclamatory (with emotion) sentences end with exclamation points.

Write an exclamation to go with each picture. Be sure to use an exclamation mark at the end of your sentences.

Which Is It?

Read each sentence below. Decide whether the sentence needs a period, question mark, or exclamation point at the end. Then write the proper punctuation at the end of each sentence.

1. Did Mrs. MacDougall send home your math work

2. My dad will bring us to soccer today

3. Sam gave me a bite of her sandwich

4. I won the game

5. What is your favorite color

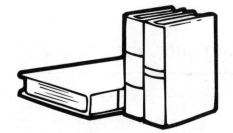

6. When is this book due at the library

7. Look out for the falling tree

8. I need to feed my dog Sparky

9. How much did the candy cost

10. That was hot

Make Your Mark

Write a sentence for each type of punctuation mark.

1. period (.)
   _____

   _____

2. question mark (?)
   _____

   _____

3. exclamation point (!)
   _____

   _____

Write each sentence with the correct punctuation mark at the end.

1. Do you know the story about the gingerbread man
   _____

   _____

   _____

2. He ran fast, but he was caught by the fox
   _____

   _____

3. What a surprise at the end
   _____

   _____

Matching Marks

Draw a line to match each sentence half. Then write each sentence below. Be sure to use the correct punctuation at the end of each sentence.

1. The bird   is my favorite food
2. Where is my   so mad
3. Hurry, the cup   flew to her nest
4. Pepperoni pizza   is falling off the table
5. That makes me   red and white baseball cap

1. _____

2. _____

3. _____

4. _____

5. _____

Make a List

Punctuation Rule: Use commas to separate items in a series.

Each box below has pictures of three items. List the items in the box in a series. Be sure to separate the items with commas.

1. _____

   _____

   _____

2. _____

   _____

   _____

3. _____

   _____

   _____

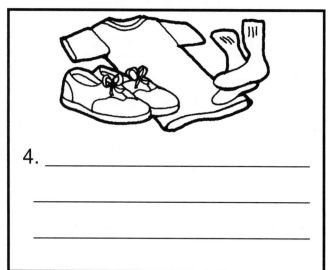

4. _____

   _____

   _____

Turn one of the lists in the boxes above into a sentence. Be sure to separate each item with a comma.

_____

_____

_____

_____

_____

The Word Series

Punctuation Rule: Use commas to separate words in a series.

Practice using commas to separate the words in each series.

1. I had chicken green beans and mashed potatoes for dinner.

2. Is your favorite sport soccer baseball or basketball?

3. We saw dolphins whales and crabs at the beach.

4. I like to play cards checkers and chess at night.

5. Would you like to swim run or bike today?

6. Did she use markers crayons or colored pencils
    to draw that picture?

7. We went to the zoo library and park over the weekend.

8. Did you see Otto Sam and Reggie at the game yesterday?

9. Ballet tap and jazz are three types of dance.

10. Swimming biking and running are all Olympic sports.

Adjectives and Nouns

Punctuation Rule: Use commas to separate adjectives (describing words) describing the same noun.

Separate the adjectives in the sentences below by putting commas in the correct places.

1. My cat has shiny black fur.

2. Miguel brought a new red bike to the playground.

3. Can you give me a bite of hot tasty pizza?

4. Mr. Waugh taught us to write long funny stories.

5. We played soccer on the wet muddy field.

Complete each sentence by writing two adjectives (describing words) in each blank. Be sure to separate adjectives with commas.

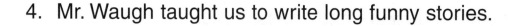

1. A _____ girl played on the team.

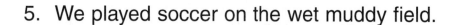

2. Do you have a _____ pencil I can borrow?

3. My mother has a _____ dress.

4. When will the _____ snow stop falling?

5. The _____ frog jumped on the lily pad.

Add a Comma

Punctuate these sentences correctly by adding commas where they are needed.

1. The long winding road made me feel carsick.

2. Melissa Hallie and Megan played on my softball team.

3. I enjoy reading writing and science in my classroom.

4. Do you have a bright red flag we can use for the game?

5. Don't forget to wash dry and brush your hair before you go to bed.

6. When will we get our blue yellow and pink paints?

7. My father Richard is tall dark and handsome.

8. Her grandma baked her a cake pie and cookies.

9. When will this hot muggy weather come to an end?

10. I walk to school with Brad Mark and Peter

Comma Time

Sets of words are in the boxes below. Choose a set of words to fit into each sentence. Be sure to use commas where they are needed.

pizza soda and candy	big red ball
sour yellow lemons	big hairy bears
dogs cats and fish	blue green and red

1. I saw _____ at the zoo.

2. We have _____ paint.

3. I played with the _____ at recess.

4. They sold _____ at the movies.

5. _____ make good pets.

6. _____ make good lemonade.

Capitalize and Punctuate

Capitals: Circle each word that should be capitalized.

1. i went to see a movie with john on saturday.

2. on tuesday we will play with ben.

3. did you go to the park in march with kara?

4. can i build a snowman in february at jim's cabin?

5. we will go to the beach in june, july, and august.

Ending Punctuation: Place the correct punctuation mark at the end of each sentence.

1. Teva and Julia are best friends

2. They like to ski in the mountains

3. Do you like to ski on the soft, white snow in December

4. Watch out for falling snow

5. What do you like to do when it snows

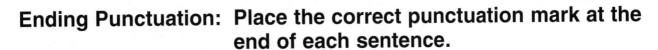

Commas: Place commas where they are needed.

1. I have a shiny orange goldfish for a pet.

2. Each morning I watch her swim glide and wiggle around her bowl.

3. Do you have a fish dog or cat as a pet?

Correct It

Change the sentences below to show the correct capitalization and punctuation rules.

Example: today i will go to my friend's house to play

T   I

~~T~~oday ~~i~~ will go to my friend's house to play.

1. i have a pet dog named lady

2. lady was born on the tenth of november

3. on tuesday we will celebrate her birthday

4. do you think it is funny to have a party for lady

5. can your dog fluffy come to the party

6. i can't wait until the party

7. should we serve cake ice cream and soda

8. on monday i will decorate the house with balloons

9. don't pop that big red balloon

10. what do you think i can do for lady in december

Make It Right

Change the sentences below to show the correct capitalization and punctuation rules.

> Example: last friday we watched a movie at the theater
>
>   L   F
>   ~~l~~ast ~~f~~riday we watched a movie at the theater.

1. my friend jose garcia likes to play soccer on saturdays

2. i like to play basketball baseball and hockey on the weekend

3. what sport would you like to play after school on thursday

4. in september soccer season begins

5. do you play soccer on a green grassy field

6. baseball is played by children teens and adults in april

7. watch out for that fly ball

8. is football shown on television monday nights

9. cheer for our team

10. does brittany like to watch football with her friend sara

Edit and Write

Rewrite the sentences below to show the correct capitalization and punctuation rules.

1. can i go to the beach on friday

2. the beach is a fun place to play in july

3. did you see that bird fly over jessica's head

4. my friend julian and i like to ride the waves

5. look out for that foaming white wave

6. what can you find at the beach in august

7. at the beach i saw sand seaweed and rocks

8. on sunday a big orange crab crawled across my towel

Unit Assessment

Shade in the bubble that completes the sentence correctly.

1. Can _____ see the book?
   - ○ a. i
   - ○ b. I
   - ○ c. me

2. _____ went to the store.
   - ○ a. me
   - ○ b. i
   - ○ c. I

3. _____ sister has a red skirt.
   - ○ a. My
   - ○ b. her
   - ○ c. my

4. ___ people like to eat pizza.
   - ○ a. some
   - ○ b. Most
   - ○ c. most

5. Give _____ the white ball.
   - ○ a. john
   - ○ b. paul
   - ○ c. Marie

6. My dog's name is _____.
   - ○ a. Fritz
   - ○ b. fluffy
   - ○ c. brownie

7. Will we sing on _____?
   - ○ a. Wednesday
   - ○ b. friday
   - ○ c. thursday

8. _____ is a holiday.
   - ○ a. friday
   - ○ b. sunday
   - ○ c. Monday

9. Thanksgiving is in _____
   - ○ a. november
   - ○ b. october
   - ○ c. November

10. In _____ we celebrate Valentine's Day.
    - ○ a. january
    - ○ b. February
    - ○ c. february

Unit Assessment *(cont.)*

Shade in the bubble that completes the sentence correctly.

11. Give that to me now__
    - ○ a. .
    - ○ b. ?
    - ○ c. !

12. I like to eat peaches__
    - ○ a. .
    - ○ b. ?
    - ○ c. !

13. Joanne is good at baseball__
    - ○ a. .
    - ○ b. ?
    - ○ c. !

14. Where is the bathroom__
    - ○ a. .
    - ○ b. ?
    - ○ c. !

15. When will the movie begin__
    - ○ a. .
    - ○ b. ?
    - ○ c. !

16. Look out for the fire__
    - ○ a. .
    - ○ b. ?
    - ○ c. !

17. We like to play _____.
    - ○ a. soccer baseball and hockey
    - ○ b. soccer, baseball, and hockey
    - ○ c. soccer baseball, and hockey

18. Do you have _____ paint?
    - ○ a. red, yellow, and blue
    - ○ b. red, yellow, and, blue
    - ○ c. red yellow and blue

19. The clown has a _____.
    - ○ a. red shiny nose
    - ○ b. red, shiny, nose
    - ○ c. red, shiny nose

20. Watch out for the _____!
    - ○ a. yellow, buzzing bees
    - ○ b. yellow, buzzing, bees
    - ○ c. yellow buzzing bees

Unit Assessment *(cont.)*

Shade in the bubble of the sentence showing the correct capitalization and punctuation.

21.

- ○ a. Today I will feed my cat Muffy.
- ○ b. today I will feed my cat Muffy?
- ○ c. today i will feed my cat muffy.

22.

- ○ a. i like to eat pizza, popcorn, and pretzels.
- ○ b. I like to eat pizza, popcorn, and pretzels.
- ○ c. I like to eat pizza popcorn and pretzels?

23.

- ○ a. will olivia ride her bike on wednesday.
- ○ b. Will Olivia ride her bike on wednesday?
- ○ c. Will Olivia ride her bike on Wednesday?

24.

- ○ a. Watch out for the fire!
- ○ b. Watch out for the fire?
- ○ c. watch out for the fire.

25.

- ○ a. my grandmother bakes pies in december!
- ○ b. My grandmother bakes pies in december?
- ○ c. My grandmother bakes pies in December.

Unit Assessment (cont.)

Shade in the bubble of the sentence showing the correct capitalization and punctuation.

26.
- ○ a. did luke eat his green beans on monday?
- ○ b. Did Luke eat his green beans on Monday?
- ○ c. did Luke eat his green beans on Monday.

27.
- ○ a. Will i wear a costume in October.
- ○ b. Will I wear a costume in October?
- ○ c. will i wear a costume in october?

28.
- ○ a. The quick, brown, fox ran to his hole?
- ○ b. the quick, brown fox ran to his hole.
- ○ c. The quick, brown fox ran to his hole.

29.
- ○ a. Throw me the ball!
- ○ b. throw me the ball!
- ○ c. throw me the ball?

30.
- ○ a. i hope jennifer douheret is my teacher.
- ○ b. I hope jennifer douheret is my teacher.
- ○ c. I hope Jennifer Douheret is my teacher.

Answer Key

Page 5
All answers: I

Page 6
1. I like to eat pizza for dinner.
2. I have a pet rat named Angel.
3. On Friday, I am going to a birthday party.
4. I learned to ride a horse when I was seven.
5. If I eat my vegetables, then I get desert.

Page 7
Answers will vary but should begin with "I like…"

Page 8
1. Today
2. We
3. Did
4. Some
5. A
6. He
7. Give
8. What

Page 9
1. We write in our spelling books.
2. Math was easy today!
3. The date is on the chalkboard.
4. Today we sang a song about the flag.
5. Did you play ball at recess?

Page 10
Wording may vary. Check to make sure the first word in each sentence begins with a capital letter.

Page 11
Wording may vary. Check to make sure the first word in each sentence begins with a capital letter.

Page 12
1. Richard
2. Kara
3. Colton
4. Jane Hill
5. Ted Lee
6. Ben Poe
7. Mary Gray
8. Sue Ann Carr
9. Pat Ward
10. Jim Roberts

Page 13
1. Linda bought some grapes at the store.
2. What did Gary do at the beach?
3. Go to the show with Matthew Morgan.
4. Kari Knowles is driving down the street.
5. My brother's name is Ethan Zane Emery.

Page 14
1. Sunday
2. Monday
3. Tuesday
4. Wednesday
5. Thursday
6. Friday
7. Saturday
Answers will vary. Check to make sure the names of the days are capitalized.

Page 15
1. I have piano lessons on Monday.
2. Saturday our family went to the beach.
3. Mark is coming over to play on Wednesday.
Answers will vary. Check to make sure the names of the days are capitalized.

Page 16
1. January
2. February
3. March
4. April
5. May
6. June
7. July
8. August
9. September
10. October
11. November
12. December

1. December, January, or February
2. March, April, or May
3. June, July, or August

Page 17
1. My birthday is in December
2. We will go to my grandma's house in May.
3. Will you take your vacation in July?
Answers will vary. Check to make sure the names of the months are capitalized.

Page 18
1. This July my family and I are taking a trip to Texas.
2. We will visit our cousins Natalie and Nile Rodgers.
3. I have already begun to plan our July vacation.
4. We will arrive Monday at Natalie and Nile's house.
5. They will take us to the zoo on Tuesday and Wednesday.
6. Then I will visit with my friend Teresa Linden on Thursday.
7. Our family will fly home on Friday.
8. Meredith Hemerson will pick us up at the airport Friday night.
9. I can't wait until July!
10. Do you think we can take one trip in November and one in May?

Page 19
1. My birthday comes each June.
2. I will go to the park on Friday.
3. Katie will call Sara on Tuesday.
4. On Thursday I will call Melanie Hart.
5. She ran on a Wednesday in August.

6. He has to work on Saturday.

Page 20
1. How, July
2. Mike, Tuesday
3. I, Rex
4. Some, Friday
5. I, Jim
6. Is, April

Page 21
All answers end with a period.
1. Our team is the Cobras.
2. We won our game.
3. I played goalie.
4. Our colors are red and black.

Page 22
Answers will vary. Check to make sure each sentence ends with a period.

Page 23
Answers will vary. Check to make sure each sentence ends with a period.

Page 24
1. A dog is in his house.
2. I ate the ice cream.
3. Sharks swim in the ocean.
4. I can read my book.
5. This is a good apple.

Page 25
1. Turn to page 25 in your book.
2. Give me the yellow ball.
3. Shut the door gently.
Answers will vary. Check to make sure the sentence is a command and that it ends with a period.

Page 26
Each sentence should end with a question mark.
1. What
2. Do
3. Will
4. Who
5. Why
6. Can
7. When
8. How
9. Does
10. Did

Page 27
Answers will vary. Check to make sure each question ends with a question mark.

Page 28
1. Who invented the light bulb? B. Thomas Edison invented the light bulb.
2. Ocean water taste salty. D. How does ocean water taste?
3. What color is a stop sign? E. A stop sign is red.

© *Teacher Created Materials, Inc.*   47   *#3344 Punctuate and Capitalize Grade 1*

Answer Key *(cont.)*

4. Thanksgiving is in November. A. When is Thanksgiving?
5. The Statue of Liberty is in New York. C. Where is the Statue of Liberty?

Answers will vary. Check to make sure there is a question mark at the end of the question sentence and a period after the answer sentence.

Page 29
1. Give the basketball to me!
2. Look out for the waterfall!
3. Be careful with that match!

Page 30
Answers will vary. Check to make sure an exclamation point is at the end of each sentence.

Page 31
1. ?
2. .
3. .
4. !
5. ?
6. ?
7. !
8. .
9. ?
10. !

Page 32
Answers will vary. Check to make sure the proper punctuation ends each sentence.
1. Do you know the story about the gingerbread man?
2. He ran fast, but he was caught by the fox.
3. What a surprise at the end!

Page 33
1. The bird flew to her nest.
2. Where is my red and white baseball cap?
3. Hurry, the cup is falling off the table!
4. Pepperoni pizza is my favorite food.
5. That makes me so mad!

Page 34
1. apple, orange, and banana
2. desk, chair, and girl
3. television, radio, and telephone
4. shoes, shirt, and socks

Sentences will vary. Check to make sure commas have been used correctly.

Page 35
1. chicken, green beans, and mashed potatoes
2. soccer, baseball, or basketball
3. dolphins, whales, and crabs
4. cards, checkers, and chess
5. swim, run, or bike
6. markers, crayons, or colored pencils
7. zoo, library, and park
8. Otto, Sam, and Reggie
9. Ballet, tap, and jazz
10. Swimming, biking, and running

Page 36
1. shiny, black fur
2. new, red bike
3. hot, tasty pizza
4. long, funny stories
5. wet, muddy field

Answers will vary. Check to make sure the comma is in the correct place.

Page 37
1. long, winding road
2. Melissa, Hallie, and Megan
3. reading, writing, and science
4. bright, red flag
5. wash, dry, and brush
6. blue, yellow, and pink
7. tall, dark, and handsome
8. cake, pie, and cookies
9. hot, muggy weather
10. Brad, Mark, and Peter

Page 38
1. big, hairy bears
2. blue, green, and red
3. big, red ball
4. pizza, soda, and candy
5. Dogs, cats, and fish.
6. sour, yellow lemons

Page 39
1. I, John, Saturday
2. On, Tuesday, Ben
3. Did, March, Kara
4. Can, I, February, Jim's
5. We, June, July, August
1. .
2. .
3. ?
4. !
5. ?
1. shiny, orange goldfish
2. swim, glide, and wiggle
3. fish, dog, or cat

Page 40
1. I have a pet dog named Lady.
2. Lady was born on the tenth of November.
3. On Tuesday we will celebrate her birthday.
4. Do you think it is funny to have a party for Lady?
5. Can your dog Fluffy come to the party?
6. I can't wait until the party!
7. Should we serve cake, ice cream, and soda?
8. On Monday I will decorate the house with balloons.
9. Don't pop that big, red balloon!
10. What do you think I can do for Lady in December?

Page 41
1. My friend Jose Garcia likes to play soccer on Saturdays.
2. I like to play basketball, baseball, and hockey on the weekend.
3. What sport would you like to play after school on Thursday?
4. In September soccer season begins.
5. Do you play soccer on a green, grassy field?
6. Baseball is played by children, teens, and adults in April.
7. Watch out for that fly ball!
8. Is football shown on television Monday nights?
9. Cheer for our team!
10. Does Brittany like to watch football with her friend Sara?

Page 42
1. Can I go to the beach on Friday?
2. The beach is a fun place to play in July.
3. Did you see that bird fly over Jessica's head?
4. My friend Julian and I like to ride the waves.
5. Look out for that foaming, white wave!
6. What can you find at the beach in August?
7. At the beach I saw sand, seaweed, and rocks.
8. On Sunday a big, orange crab crawled across my towel.

Page 43-46
1. b
2. c
3. a
4. b
5. c
6. a
7. a
8. c
9. c
10. b
11. c
12. a
13. a
14. b
15. b
16. c
17. b
18. a
19. c
20. a
21. a
22. b
23. c
24. a
25. c
26. b
27. b
28. c
29. a
30. c